To:

_____

From:

_____

I'll love you forever.
I'll like you for always.
As long as I'm living my baby you'll be.
~ From "Love You Forever," by Robert Munsch

NOTES TO MY BABY

I Love You Already

Vesna M. Bailey

OMNI Publishing
Leamington, Ontario, Canada

Dedication

For Karyn, Lauren, and Stephen —
I love you so much, and
I can't imagine my world without you.

To my beautiful Karyn,
You are my youngest,
you will always be my baby.
Thank-you for letting me cuddle with you,
well beyond your bedtime,
thank-you for letting me keep kissing you
well beyond your years,
you just seemed to know how I wanted to keep you
my baby,
well beyond the seasons of time,
and now I see that my baby
is at home in my heart
forever.

~ I Love You, Mom

Catch me a rainbow,
a rainbow to keep,
so I can dream pretty colored dreams,
and with gladness awaken and breathe;
so I can dine with kings and queens,
and with paupers and shepherds,
so I can yell out, in a voice of every color,
"Just you wait and see all that I can be,
all that I will be,
just you wait and see,
don't take your eyes off of me!"

Contents

Forever Two (Introduction)   11

Dear Baby   14

The Wonder of You   17

Already I Know   31

I Can't Wait   39

Soon You Will See   57

If I Could Have It All My Way For You   71

I Promise You   91

Mother: the most beautiful
word on the lips of mankind.
~ Kahil Gibran

Forever Two

(Introduction)

How can the heart keep aside so much room for something that one day is not there, and then in the flash of a moment, it becomes paramount to everything in one's heart, in one's life? I don't know. When I myself experienced it, I remember thinking, there are no words – this is unexplainable, and indescribable, until it happens to you. It is like the heart is a knowing, devoted keeper of the most beautiful secret, so extraordinary in its reach that it is unimaginable until that precise moment when one discovers she will be a mother. There is a shift and a transformation in us like no other we have ever known; as with the surge of the most thunderous lightning bolt, a new meaning is at once infused into everything we see, and touch, and feel; this new life inside us becomes our purpose. It is nothing short of miraculous that all this can happen in one instant. In a way, it is like we ourselves are newly born, and as of then, we mothers, begin living forever as two, for two; mother and child. It is no wonder that motherhood is the single most universal, and the most unifying, element in all the world. Regardless of age, or race, or religious convictions, when a mother sees another mother with her child, she can instantly feel everything another mother is feeling ... whether it is of tragedy, or of happiness, we know ... we just know ... we know because we share the same mothers' heartbeat, we know what it is to be living for two.

I wrote this book because I am grateful. I am grateful for so many things in my life, but most of all I am grateful for the privilege I have had to be a Mom to three amazing children. I remember the moment "I knew" for each of them, and each time it was like a new miracle, while at the same time it was the very same miracle. I love my three children no more, and no less, than every mother loves their child. I recently found myself deeply inspired to reflect on, and to write down, the thoughts, the feelings, and the aspirations that filled my heart and mind during those magical first nine months when I was preparing for the birth of each of my children, and when the world was preparing for them as well. I know these pages are not my own; they speak to the defining fibre of every mother, and they have been written in the skies and the stars from the beginning of time.

As you find yourself perusing through these pages here, I want to say to you, it is a joy, and it is a privilege, to celebrate your extraordinary journey with you: for all the days of your life, you will now be travelling as two! In reading the words here, I hope you will be inspired to add your own notes which will, for your baby, be a mirror on your mother's-heart-in-waiting always – it will be your child's "back story" … a back story like no other. During this amazing time of preparation, there is so much to tell a child – about you, about the baby's father, about your family, about your hopes and convictions … you are preparing the way for your baby, layering it with all the faces of a mother's love.

I wish you and your growing baby good health and happiness always. Rest assured, life is good, life is full of miracles, life is beautiful, and you will be an amazing Mom … you already are!!

> I love you already
> because you are mine,
> and I am yours,
> I love you already,
> I just do.
> ~ Love, Mom

Dear Baby,

The WONDER of YOU ...

Piglet: How do you spell love?
Pooh: You don't spell it, you feel it.
~ from "Winnie the Pooh," by A.A. Milne

It takes my breath away to think that it's not all just make believe,
you really are mine,
soon you will be here, and …
I will be your Mommy!

I love it when you nudge me,
for then I know all is as it should be,
you are safe and sound, and
miracles are true and real.

If you only knew how much time I spend imagining you,
imagining how perfect and beautiful I know you will be.
Oh, how I wonder about so many things, like
are you a boy,
are you a girl,
is your hair light or dark, straight or curly,
how will you show your little personality,
how will your voice sound when you say, "mama,"
how will your giggles sound,
how will your delicate skin feel when I lay you on my bosom?

I don't know enough words,
I don't know enough numbers,
I don't know enough colors,
I don't know how to describe it,
I just know it is my love
for you.
It was there before I even knew you.

~ Love, Mom

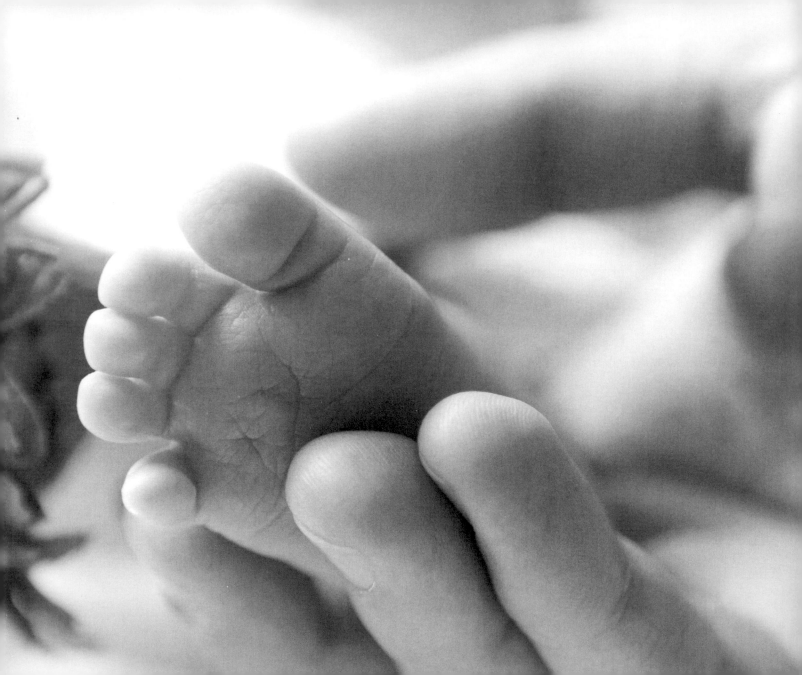

There seems to be no end to my wonder … tell me,
who is the little person I will discover inside you,
who will you grow to be,
how will you paint the world …
what beautiful things are sure to come because of you?

I cannot wait to know you.
Every time I think of you,
I love you in a thousand more ways —
you would not think that is possible,
but it is.

> I cannot wait to love you
> every minute,
> every day,
> every kiss,
> for the rest of my days.
>
> ~ Love, Mom

Sometimes I get scared that I will not know how to do
everything well, but
I am reading, and listening, and
trying to do everything right so you grow healthy and strong.
My friends and family keep telling me that once I have you,
my life, my world, will change forever,
all good I know.
I think I am one of the lucky ones,
already I am blessed with so many of life's blessings, and
that makes me want you in my life even more, and
it makes me feel sure I am truly ready for you.

I cannot wait to begin our incredible journey together.
Planning to have you is my life's greatest undertaking,
raising you will be my greatest achievement, and
without a doubt, I know
your birth will be one of the greatest moments of my life.

I have been thinking about the best things and the most
important things in life
that I want to share with you,
that I want to say to you,
that I hope for you,
things I want you to know,
and so many important things which I expect of myself –
I noted some of them on these next pages here.

Until I see you,
just know
I want to be the best Mommy I can be to you,
I will take good care of you,
I will do my best to raise you to be kind, to be happy, and
to be everything you can be.
I hope to make you always very, very proud
to have me for your Mommy.
The wonder of you has filled my world to the brim already, and
you must know,

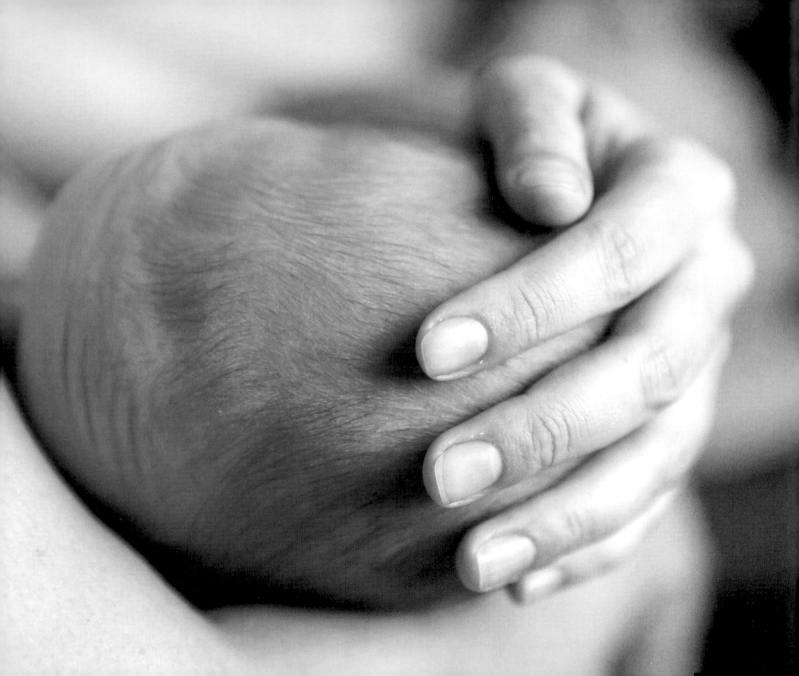

I love you already.

"Piglet sidled up to Pooh from behind. 'Pooh?' he whispered. 'Yes, Piglet?' 'Nothing,' said Piglet, taking Pooh's hand. I just wanted to be sure of you.'"
~ *from "Winnie the Pooh," by A.A. Milne*

Already
I KNOW ...

You are the only ONE you –
the world over, there has never been anyone else like you.
You are perfect as you are,
as perfect as perfect can be!

Already
I KNOW ...

There is only one pretty child in the world, and every mother has it.

~ Chinese Proverb

You are beautiful.

You are smart.

You are strong.

Already
I KNOW ...

The world will be a better place because of you.

My life is blessed because you are mine.

> Take courage and be you,
> all the world is more special —
> because already you are you.
>
> ~ Love, Mom

Already

I KNOW ...

I CAN'T
wait to ...

"I'll Eat You Up I Love You So"
~ *from "Where the Wild Things Are," by Maurice Sendak*

I can't wait to kiss you.

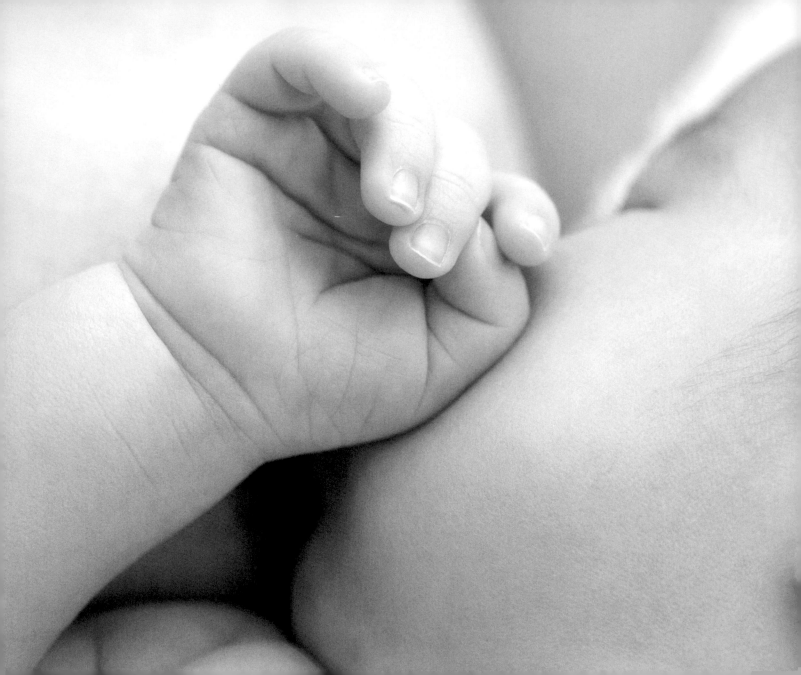

I CAN'T
wait to ...

I can't wait to lay you on my chest,
I can't wait to feel the sweetness of your breath,
I can't wait to just hold you.

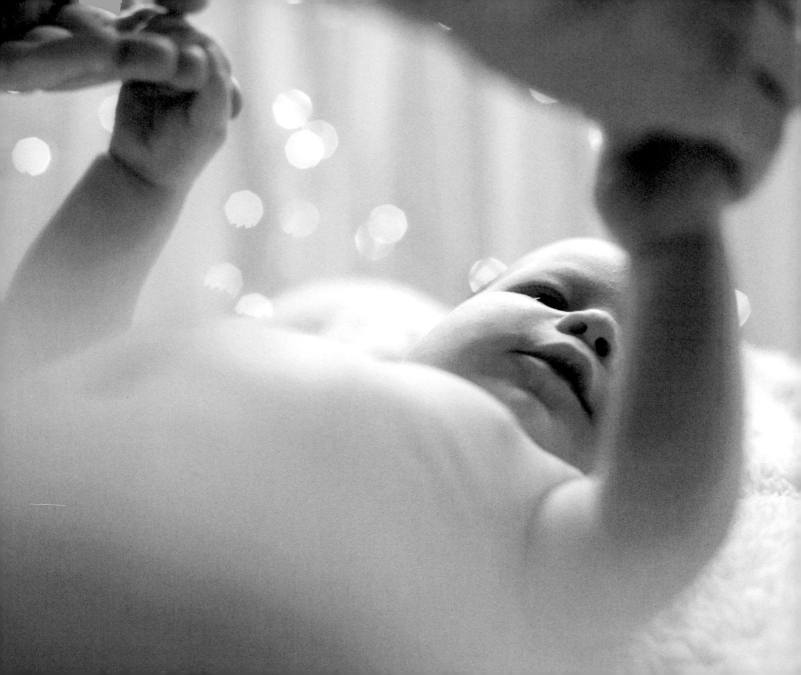

I CAN'T
wait to ...

I can't wait to call you by your name.

> I want to hold your little hand,
> I want to play with you in the sand,
> I want to take you by the hand,
> to all the places where happy grows.
>
> ~ Love, Mom

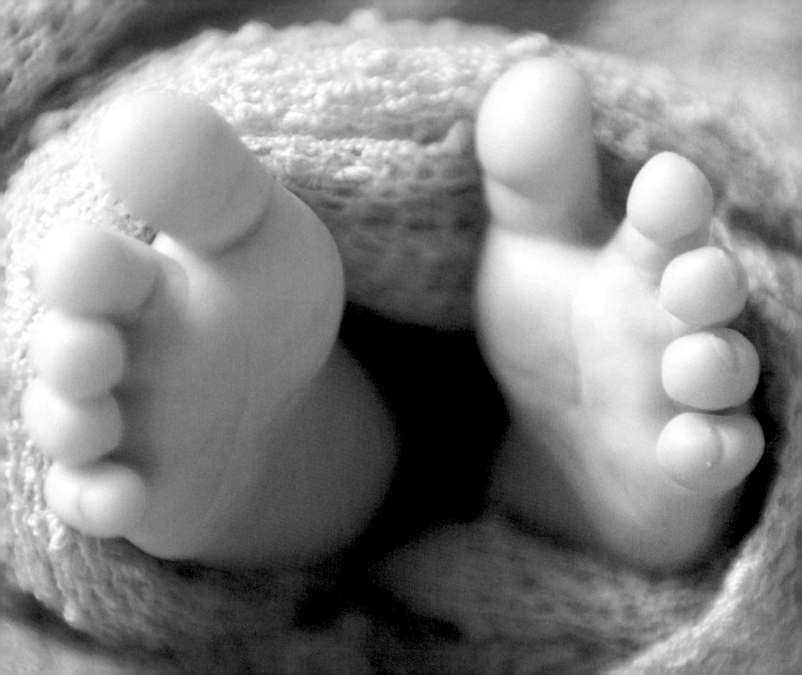

I CAN'T wait to ...

"Life Will Never Be The Same Because There Had Never Been Anyone Like You...Ever in the World."
~ *from "On the Night You Were Born," by Nancy Tillman.*

I can't wait to brush my cheek against your soft skin,

I can't wait to run my fingers through your hair.

I can't wait to count your fingers and your toes,

I can't wait to tickle you,

I can't wait to see your little kicks and wiggles,

I can't wait to watch you sleep,

I can't wait to be there each time you wake up.

I CAN'T
wait to ...

Mother: She never quite leaves her children at home, even when she doesn't take them along.

~ *Margaret Culkin Banning*

I can't wait to hold your hand,
I can't wait to grow with you,
I can't wait to learn from you.

I CAN'T
wait to ...

I can't wait to see the pictures you will draw —
a house, a cat, a flower, our family, …
what else will you love to draw?

> Let's go kiss the sky,
> let's go see how bumpy all the clouds are,
> let's go swinging through the jungle deep,
> let's go wake all the froggies from their sleep,
> let's come home when we are tired,
> to lay down on our best soft pillow.
>
> ~ Love, Mom

I CAN'T
wait to ...

I can't wait to read your favourite story to you,
the same one over and over I know it will be.

I can't wait to discover your favourite rhyme,
the one that will make you laugh and giggle every time,
… will it be, This Little Piggy Went To the Market,
or will it be, Eensy Weensy Spider?
Or, will it be another?

Can I really catch a star?
And keep it in my pocket for always?
Yes, why not …
everyone can have a pocket star.
Hmmmmm … that's good to know.

~ Love, Mom

I CAN'T
wait to ...

"Sometimes, I've believed as many as six impossible things before breakfast."

~ *from "Alice's Adventures in Wonderland," by Lewis Carroll*

I can't wait to count stars in the night sky with you,
to watch you dream about touching the moon,
to together look for dragons and all sorts of creatures in
the clouds,
to see your sand castles that I know will be the envy of all
kingdoms yet.

I CAN'T
wait to ...

SOON YOU will see ...

"To Live Would Be An Awfully Big Adventure."
~ from "Pater Pan," by J.M. Barrie

The world truly is so amazing,
I can't wait to show it all to you,
oh, what an adventure you are about to begin —
all the corners of the world that you will find,
all the places in the heart that you will travel,
all the loves that you will know,
soon you will see.

SOON YOU will see ...

There are kind people everywhere,
soon you will see.

There are such beautiful and magical places in the world,
so many,
soon you will see.

> Close your eyes,
> soar and fly,
> from head to toe now believe it –
> this is how all little boys and girls
> grow their wings,
> and learn to fly.
>
> ~ Love, Mom

SOON YOU will see ...

The oceans are filled with the most beautiful things …
fish of all colors, magical shells,
even star fish and sand dollars,
soon you will see.

SOON YOU will see ...

"Believing takes practice."
~ from "A Wrinkle in Time," by Madeliene L'Engle

The mountains are so big and tall,
and there are secrets that echo from peak to peak,
you will hear them,
soon you will see.

SOON YOU will see ...

'Real isn't how you are made,' said the Skin Horse. 'It's a thing that happens to you. "When a child loves you for a long, long time, not just to play with, but REALLY loves you, then you become Real."

~ from "The Velveteen Rabbit," by Margery Williams

And did I tell you about all the magic?
There is so much coming your way …
there is the loveable Frosty,
then there is Santa –
he lives in the North Pole, and that's all I will tell you about him for now.
Then there is the Tooth Fairy …
but you will have to wait for a while and sleep tight to get a visit from her.
There is just so much more,
too much to fit it all into this little spot here,
but trust in me, you will love it all,
soon you will see.

SOON YOU will see ...

A big, beautiful world is waiting for you,
soon you will see.

All the world is preparing,
busy bees gathering their sweetest honey,
tiny ants, big ants, all building hills so high,
streets from north to south, from east to west,
now parading in thousands of blossoms each –
awaiting
you.

~ Love, Mom

SOON YOU
will see ...

If I Could Have it ALL My Way for You

I hope ...

I hope you will always and forever be surrounded by love, that you will love, and be loved.

I hope you will always be blessed with good health.

> Wish loudly,
> Wish softly,
> Wish truly.
>
> ~ Love, Mom

I hope ...

"It has been a terrible, horrible, no good, very bad day.
My mom says some days are like that. Even in Australia."
~ from "Alexander and the Terrible, Horrible, No Good, Very Bad Day," by Judith Viorst

I hope you will be happy. Always.

I hope ...

But the children knew, as I'm sure you know, that the worst
surroundings in the world can be tolerated if the people in them
are interesting and kind.

-- from "The Bad Beginning," by Lemony Snicker

I hope you will see the world to be beautiful,
and that you will look for the world to be a bright and
wondrous place,
especially in those times when the clouds roll in.
It's important.

I hope ...

"UNLESS someone like you cares a whole awful lot, nothing is
going to get better. It's not."
~ from "The Lorax," by Dr. Seuss

I hope you will always know goodness and kindness,
that you will recognize it when it's there, and
will for kindness and compassion to show itself wherever needed
in those times when it is yet to come.

I hope you will always care.

I hope ...

I hope you will always have a best friend,

one that you can always count on.

I hope ...

"You Are Braver Than You Believe, stronger than you seem, smarter than you think, and loved more than you'll ever know."
~ *from "Winnie-the-Pooh," by A.A. Milne*

I hope you will always believe in yourself.
I hope you will always know,
no matter what,
you are strong and capable,
and so worthy of all your small and big dreams.
I hope you always possess a spirit that cannot be crushed.

Dream big, dream small,
everything can be,
a frog can turn into a prince,
a pumpkin into a horse-drawn carriage,
and impossible things into possible things,
everything can be,
believe it all,
because believing truly is all up to you,
and so,
in yourself you must believe most of all.

~ Love, Mom

81

I hope ...

It is our choices, Harry, that show what we truly are, far more than our abilities.

~ from "Harry Potter and the Chamber of Secrets," by J.K. Rowling

I hope you will for yourself always set your standards high,
take responsibility for your actions and your feelings, and
I hope you will strive to live up to your potential,
with a conviction, and work ethic that knows no barriers,
and no bounds.

I hope ...

"What if Christmas, he thought, doesn't come from a store. What if Christmas ... perhaps ... means a little bit more!"
~ from "How the Grinch Stole Christmas," by Dr. Seuss

I hope you will always have the courage
to choose all those things
which mirror respect and integrity.

I hope you will always know how much you matter,
how much everyone, and everything, matters,
and I hope you will always be driven to live a life that matters.

I hope ...

"Only with the Heart Can One See Rightly. What is Essential is Invisible to the Eye."

~ *from "The Little Prince," by Antoine de Saint Exupéry*

I hope you will be lucky enough to live in a peaceful world.

I hope ...

I promise
YOU ...

"I Love You Right Up To The Moon — And Back."
~ from "Guess How Much I Love You," by Sam McBratney

I will love you.
Always.

I promise
YOU ...

"Listen to the mustn'ts, child. Listen to the don'ts. Listen to the shouldn'ts, the impossibles, the won'ts. Listen to the never haves, then listen close to me ... Anything can happen, child. Anything can be."

~ from "Where the Sidewalk Ends," by Shel Silverstein

I will take care of you.
Always.

I promise
YOU ...

No language can express the power and beauty and heroism
of a mother's love.

~ Edwin H Chapin

I will protect you.
Always.

I promise
YOU ...

"A Person Is A Person, No Matter How Small."

~ from "Horton Hears a Who," by Dr. Seuss

I will respect you.
Always.

I will listen
to your words, and
to your heart.
Always.

I prom'se
YOU ...

A little girl, asked where her home was, replied,
"where mother is."

~ Keith L. Brooks

I will kiss the scrapes on your knee, and
I will always do my best to make it all better.

I promise
YOU ...

You know that place between sleep and awake...the place where you can still remember dreaming?
That's where I'll always love you. That's where I'll be waiting.
~ from "Peter Pan," by J.M. Barrie

I will kiss you good night every night,
"Sweet dreams. Don't let the bed bugs bite," I might say, and you won't know it,
but my lips on your forehead will each time
be a prayer to keep you safe for another day, and
to say the deepest thank-you for today.

I promise
YOU ...

"We all can dance," he said, "if we find the music that we love."
~ from "Giraffes Can't Dance," by Giles Andreae

I will let you be you,
I will encourage you to be you, and
let you dress always in the seasons of your heart -
even when the colours don't match!

I promise YOU ...

I will buy you sidewalk chalk and crayons,
I will frame all your Picasso drawings,
I will write your letters to Santa exactly as you say them,
I will help you learn to tie your shoes,
I will help you learn to do all sorts of things all by yourself,
... and I promise I will try to be patient!

I promise
YOU ...

Mother love is the fuel that enables a normal human being to do the impossible.

~ Marion C. Garretty

I will believe in you,
I will encourage you, I will cheer for you.
Always.

I will hold you to the highest standard;
to work hard,
to do your best,
and be your best,
always.

I promise
YOU ...

I will give you room to make your own mistakes,
those are by far the best of the lessons to be learned, and
as you will see,
those lessons can never be unlearned.

I promise
YOU ...

I will say, "I am sorry," whenever I am wrong.

I promise
YOU ...

"Generally, by the time you are Real, most of your hair has been loved off, and your eyes drop out and you get loose in the joints and very shabby. But these things don't matter at all, because once you are Real you can't be ugly, except to people who don't understand."

~ from "The Velveteen Rabbit," by Margery Williams

I will do my best to show you that the world is a glory worthy place to be…
that there is beauty to be found in everyone we meet,
and in everything we see.

I promise
YOU ...

"If You Love to be A Hundred, I Want to Live to be A Hundred Minus One Day So I Never Have to Live Without You."
~ *from "Winnie-the-Pooh," by A.A. Milne*

More than anything,
I will do my very best to show you that love matters
more than anything.

I promise
YOU ...

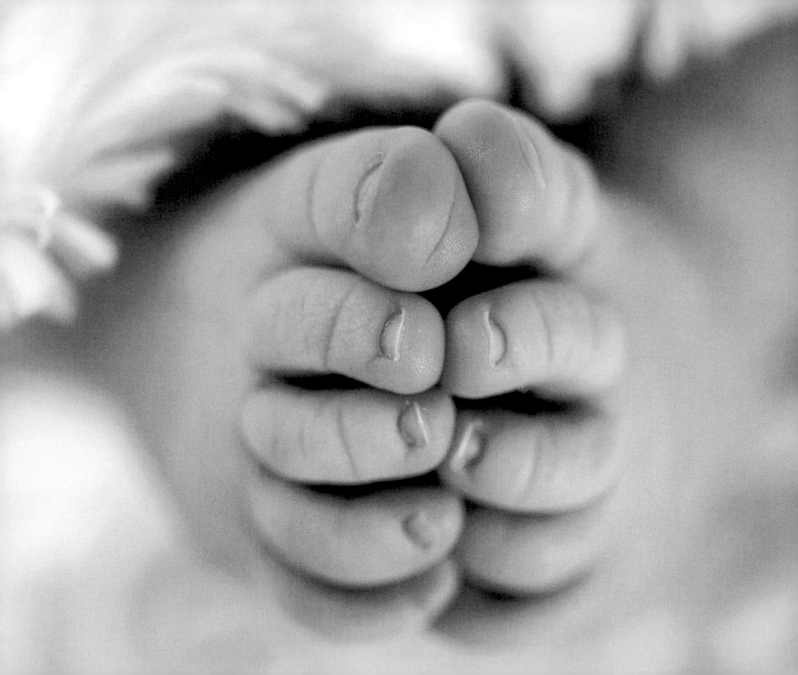

Well, this is a lot of words so far,

but truly I don't know enough words to say everything there is to say
at a time like this,

for now, the most important thing you must know is ...

I love you already.

I love you forever.

"If There Ever Comes a Day We Can't Be Together...
...keep me in your heart, I'll stay there forever."

~ from "Winnie the Pooh," by A.A. Milne

NOTES

It matters.
You matter.
Live a life that matters.

~ Mom

I love you.

About the Author

Vesna Bailey was born in Dubrovnik, Croatia and came to Canada as a child. She now lives in Leamington, Ontario, with her husband. Vesna's passion for writing is inspired by their three children, Stephen, Lauren and Karyn; being their Mom is an unparalleled joy in her life. Prior to embarking upon writing, Vesna enjoyed a rewarding career as a Speech-Language Pathologist. Her first book, *NOTES TO MY SON - Before You Go,* won a 2008 IPPY Book Award, and was awarded First Place in the 16th Annual Writer's Digest International Self-Published Writing Competition, Inspirational Category. One year later, *NOTES TO MY DAUGHTER - Before You Go,* won the same IPPY Medal. Vesna is thrilled to share her newest, long awaited labour of love, *NOTES TO MY BABY - I Love You Already.* As is mirrored in her words, as well as the photography she chooses for her gift books, she has always believed in approaching all life with inspiration for all that is good and beautiful, and all that is worthy of the best self within each of us. The power of mothering, the power of inspiring our children, the power of inspiring parents, is in full celebration throughout each of her gift books.

Much more writing is in Vesna's future plans. Her newest passion for cupcakes, from scratch, is surprising her … and her children!!

Also by Vesna M. Bailey

NOTES TO MY DAUGHTER BEFORE YOU GO

Independent Publisher Book Awards 2009
Bronze Medal Winner – Inspirational category

NOTES TO MY SON BEFORE YOU GO

Multiple Book Award Winner –

Independent Publisher Book Awards 2008
Bronze Medal Winner – Gift/Holiday/Specialty category

16th Annual Writer's Digest International Self-Published Book Awards
1st Place Winner – Inspirational category

NOTES TO MY BABY: I LOVE YOU ALREADY

www.NotesBeforeYouGo.com

Published by **OMNI Publishing**
30 Lathrop Lane, Leamington ON Canada N8H 4B4
e-mail: vesna.bailey@notesbeforeyougo.com

First Printing – Spring, 2017
all rights reserved

ISBN: 978-0-9810173-3-4

Printed in China